A LOOK AT US HISTORY

THE INDUSTRIAL REVOLUTION

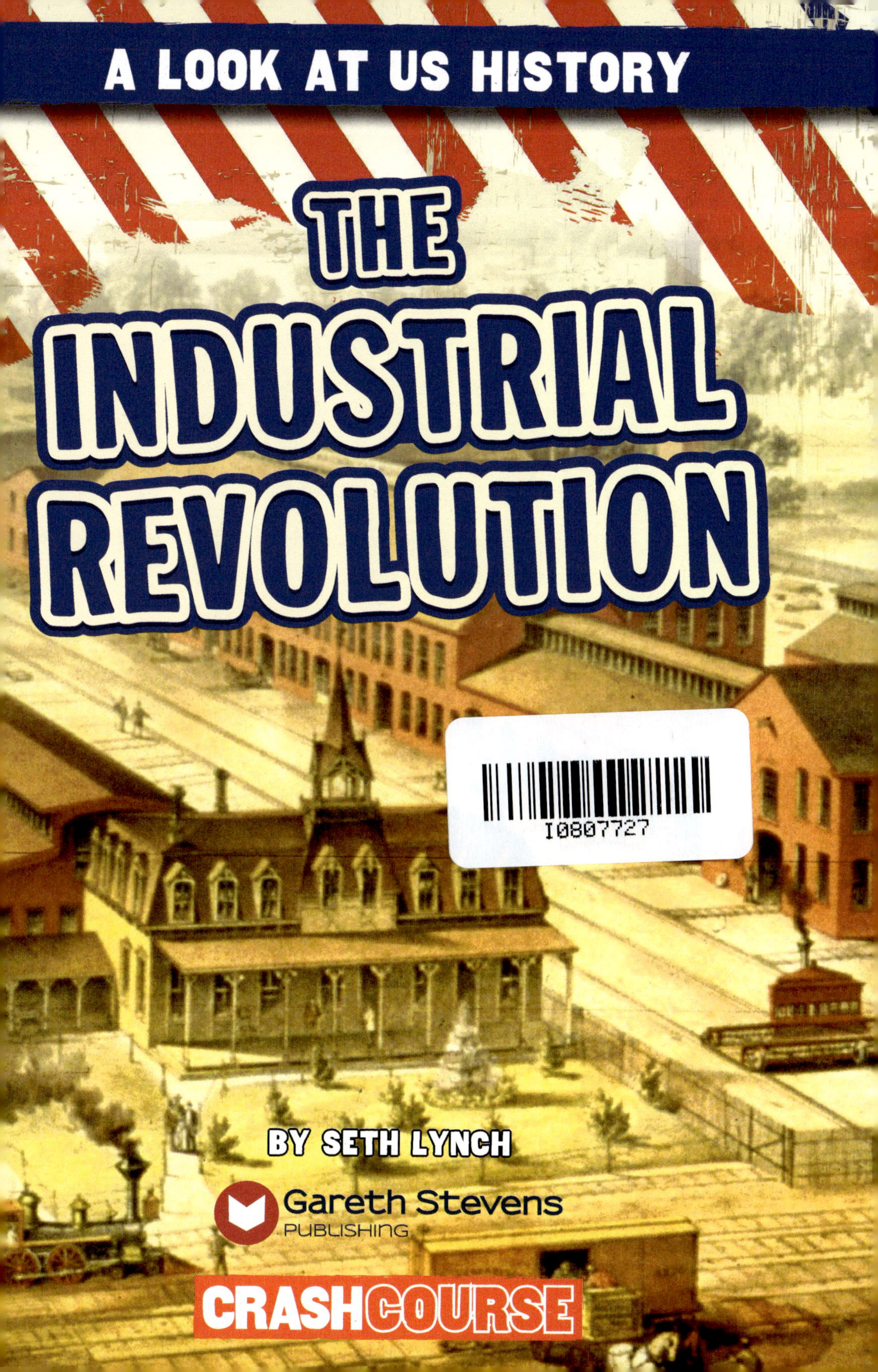

BY SETH LYNCH

Gareth Stevens PUBLISHING

CRASHCOURSE

Please visit our website, www.garethstevens.com. For a free color catalog of all our high-quality books, call toll free 1-800-542-2595 or fax 1-877-542-2596.

Cataloging-in-Publication Data

Names: Lynch, Seth.
Title: The Industrial Revolution / Seth Lynch.
Description: New York : Gareth Stevens Publishing, 2019. | Series: A look at US history | Includes index.
Identifiers: LCCN ISBN 9781538221297 (pbk.) | ISBN 9781538221273 (library bound) | ISBN 9781538221303 (6 pack)
Subjects: LCSH: Industrial revolution--United States--Juvenile literature. | Industries--United States--History--Juvenile literature. | Technological innovations--Social aspects--United States--History--Juvenile literature. | United States--Economic conditions--Juvenile literature.
Classification: LCC HC105.L96 2019 | DDC 330.973'08--dc23

First Edition

Published in 2019 by
Gareth Stevens Publishing
111 East 14th Street, Suite 349
New York, NY 10003

Designer: Samantha DeMartin
Editor: Kristen Nelson

Photo credits: Series art Christophe BOISSON/Shutterstock.com; (feather quill) Galushko Sergey/Shutterstock.com; (parchment) mollicart-design/Shutterstock.com; cover, p. 1 MPI/Archive Photos/Getty Images; p. 5 (both) Print Collector/Hulton Archive/Getty Images; p. 7 K-Smile love/Shutterstock.com; p. 9 (top) Bettmann/Bettmann/Getty Images; p. 9 (bottom) duncan1890/DigitalVision Vectors/Getty Images; p. 11 Dan Logan/Shutterstock.com; pp. 13, 23, 25 (bottom), 27 (both) Everett Historical/Shutterstock.com; pp. 15, 19, 21 Universal History Archive/Universal Images Group/Getty Images; p. 17 Culture Club/Hulton Archive/Getty Images; p. 25 (map) courtesy of Library of Congress; p. 29 Michael L. Kaufman/Wikimedia Commons.

Printed in the United States of America

CPSIA compliance information: Batch #CS18GS: For further information contact Gareth Stevens, New York, New York at 1-800-542-2595.

CONTENTS

Words in the glossary appear in **bold** type the first time they are used in the text.

FROM FARMS TO FACTORIES

The Industrial Revolution is a time period in world and US history in which the **economy** of many countries changed from being based on agriculture to being based on industry. This changed the lives of people around the world, including those in the United States, forever.

MAKE THE GRADE

Agriculture is the practice of farming, including growing food and raising animals. Industry includes manufacturing, or making, many goods at once, especially in factories.

START OVERSEAS

The Industrial Revolution began in Great Britain during the mid-1700s. Two inventions marked this beginning: the spinning jenny and the **improved** steam **engine**. The spinning jenny is a machine that spins many balls of thread or yarn at the same time. It made cloth making faster.

MAKE THE GRADE

At first, Great Britain didn't want to share their manufacturing knowledge. They knew they had an economic edge over other countries.

spinning jenny

The first steam engines were created in the late 1600s and early 1700s. By the 1760s, James Watt had made it better. His improvements made the engine more **efficient**. Steam engines would soon power the new trains, boats, and factories of the Industrial Revolution!

MAKE THE GRADE

By the early 1800s, British businessmen saw manufacturing possibilities in other European countries. They brought the Industrial Revolution to places such as Belgium. It would spread as far as Japan!

EARLY INDUSTRY IN THE UNITED STATES

Englishman Samuel Slater made the first move toward an industrial revolution in the United States. He memorized plans for British **textile** machines and built a cotton mill in Rhode Island. By 1790, it was in use. Slater's cotton mill was the first factory in the United States.

MAKE THE GRADE

Like many early US factories, Slater's cotton mill was powered by water. Many factories were built in the Northeast at first because of easy access to water for this power.

Eli Whitney invented the cotton gin in 1793. The cotton gin cleaned cotton by removing its seeds. This invention had a great economic effect. It was part of how cotton was able to become such an important crop in the South.

MAKE THE GRADE

As the cotton economy grew, so did the need for slaves in the South.

Some of the machines that truly changed America were those made for farms. Between 1797 and the 1830s, many plows were **patented**. These and other machinery allowed farmers to produce more crops for less money. Many farmworkers lost their jobs to these new machines.

MAKE THE GRADE

New mines opened across the United States as more **natural resources**, such as coal, were needed to make and power machinery. Some people in need of work found jobs in these mines.

THE BIG MOVE

Many out-of-work farmworkers headed to cities to find new jobs in factories. Cities like Boston, Massachusetts; Chicago, Illinois; and New York City grew because of this. As the Industrial Revolution went on, millions of people would leave farming communities for new city centers.

MAKE THE GRADE

Farmworkers commonly didn't need special skills to work in mills and factories. While this made it easier to find work, the unskilled jobs were often boring and **repetitive**.

POST-WAR GROWTH

Cities grew even more after the **Civil War**. About 25 million **immigrants** moved to the United States between 1866 and 1915. Many came from Europe and settled in big cities. They saw the United States' new industries as opportunities for work and a better life.

MAKE THE GRADE

Coming to the United States didn't improve many immigrants' lives. With all the new people, cities quickly became overcrowded. Good housing wasn't available for everyone.

Those who had been slaves also came to the growing cities of the North following the Civil War. They were treated better there and escaped problems with Southerners who had fought against their freedom. Factory jobs helped them start new lives as full US citizens.

MAKE THE GRADE

Slaves who headed north for jobs in cities didn't want to become **sharecroppers** under their former masters.

HARD WORK, HARD LIFE

Factory workers spent long hours in poor working **conditions**. Some of the work was quite unsafe. Until the 1930s, children often worked in factories to earn money for their families. They didn't go to school or have much time for fun.

MAKE THE GRADE

By the early 1900s, many factory workers had come together to form unions. Unions are groups that work with factory bosses for better pay, hours, and working conditions for workers.

THE BEST OF THE REVOLUTION

The Industrial Revolution changed the lives of US citizens. Some changes were bad, such as the rise of poor living conditions in cities. Others were good. Travel, for example, greatly improved during this time. Railroads crisscrossed the country, making it easier to move people and goods.

MAKE THE GRADE

Mass-produced goods, or those created in large numbers, started to take the place of homemade goods in homes. Steamboats on rivers and the new railroads were needed to ship these items.

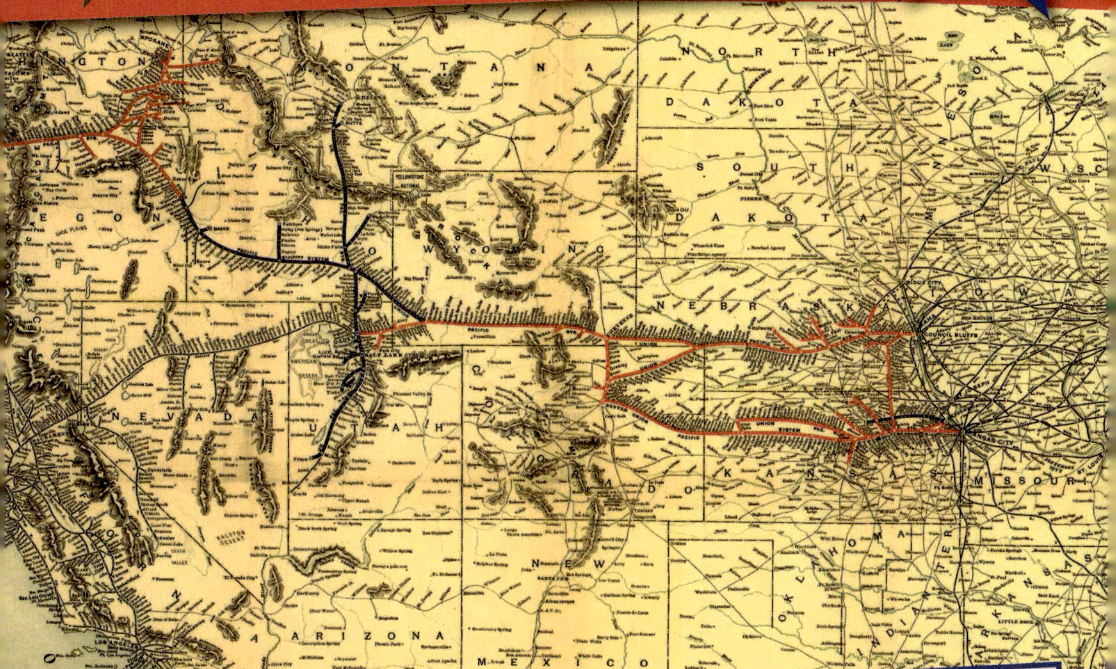

Communication became better than ever during the Industrial Revolution. The first telegraph message was sent in 1844. Alexander Graham Bell patented the telephone in 1876. By 1915, telephone calls across the country were possible!

MAKE THE GRADE

Electricity became part of life through the work of Thomas Edison and others during the Industrial Revolution. About half of Americans had electricity in their homes by 1925.

Alexander Graham Bell

Thomas Edison

The Industrial Revolution was marked by changes in the US economy, growth in cities, and great inventions. The first successful airplane flight, the building of a railroad across North America, and the manufacturing of the first cars all happened then!

MAKE THE GRADE

One important invention of the Industrial Revolution was the sewing machine. It saved time and made mass-produced clothing possible.

TIMELINE OF THE INDUSTRIAL REVOLUTION

1712
The first modern steam engine is invented.

1760s
James Watt improves the steam engine.

1770
The spinning jenny is patented.

1790
The first factory opens in the United States.

1793
Eli Whitney invents the cotton gin.

1830s
Farm machinery begins replacing workers.

1844
The first telegraph message is sent.

1861–1865
The American Civil War is fought.

1866
Freed slaves and immigrants start heading to growing American cities.

1869
The transcontinental, or cross-country, railroad is finished.

1876
The telephone is patented.

GLOSSARY

Civil War: a war fought from 1861 to 1865 in the United States between the Union (the Northern states) and the Confederacy (the Southern states)

communication: the act of using words to give and receive information

condition: the state of something

economy: the money made in an area and how it is made

efficient: the state of being the least wasteful

engine: a machine that makes power

immigrant: one who comes to a country to settle there

improve: to make better

natural resource: something in nature that can be used by people

patent: to have a piece of paper from the government that gives a person the rights to a design, machine, or process for a time

repetitive: having actions that happen again and again in a way that is boring

sharecropper: a farmer who works land owned by a landlord and earns a certain share of the crops raised

textile: woven or knit cloth

FOR MORE INFORMATION

Books

Hubbard, Ben. *Stories of Women During the Industrial Revolution: Changing Roles, Changing Lives*. Chicago, IL: Heinemann-Raintree, 2015.

Wolfe, James. *The Industrial Revolution: Steam and Steel*. New York, NY: Britannica Educational Publishing, 2016.

Website

Important Inventions of the Industrial Revolution
www.brighthubeducation.com/history-homework-help/91805-important-inventions-of-the-industrial-revolution/
Read about the amazing things created during this time period.

Publisher's note to educators and parents: Our editors have carefully reviewed this website to ensure that they are suitable for students. Many websites change frequently, however, and we cannot guarantee that a site's future contents will continue to meet our high standards of quality and educational value. Be advised that students should be closely supervised whenever they access the internet.

INDEX